Color of My Living Heart

Poems
by
Floyd Salas

Arte Público Press
Houston, Texas
1996

This volume is made possible through grants from the National Endowment for the Arts (a federal agency), Andrew W. Mellon Foundation, The Cultural Arts Council of Houston and the Lila Wallace Reader's-Digest Fund.

Recovering the past, creating the future

Arte Público Press
University of Houston
Houston, Texas 77204-2090

Cover art and design by Mark Piñón

Salas, Floyd. 1931–
Color of my living heart / by Floyd Salas.
p. cm.
ISBN 1-55885-171-2 (alk. paper)
1. Mexican Americans–Poetry. I. Title.
PS3569.A459C65 1996
811'.54–dc20 96-14245
CIP

The paper used in this publication meets the requirements of the American National Standard for Permanence of Paper for Printed Library Materials Z39.48-1984. ∞

For Leslie Woodd

Contents

Color of My Living Heart

This Is the Heart of the Apple

Whole heartedly she says
and turns her face away
This is my love
This is the heart of the apple
This is the core of my heart
This is my love

Not unless it's whole
heartedly
and turns her face away

Somewhere the pain swirls in currents of blood
her breath fogs with hurt
small mouth opens and curls

This is my love
She turns her face away

Deep in the shadow of her eye
in the green light that turns there
I hear her voice

"Put your hand in your shirt pocket
touch the wound
small sting of salt on blood
taste it

Sweeter than syrup
or strawberry jam
this is my love
this is my sweet heart
whole
heartedly"

Love me
only me
it says

Voice of heart and feeling
heart of her voice
call to me
love me

The rock
dissolves
with tears
just one at a time
for a thousand years
The rock
dissolves
with tears

There's a Narcotic Hum in the Air

A trail of ants crosses my window pane
They scurry from leaf to leaf
sill to sill
across the blue flat of space
fragile as glass
A breath will blow them away

I wait for the big black spider
back up
like a dome
swollen with the juice of his poisons
to creep out of the tent of a leaf
pop out of the dark in a hole
and pin pricks for eyes
and tusks of ivory
glide down an invisible wire
and pounce on me

I huddle in the nest of her sex
warm folds of love
that wrap me round
clutch at me
suck me in
kiss me
hold me
in prison
in the hollow of her arm
under the covers
fake sleep
to escape a bed check

The matron will pass by
She will nod her head and let me sleep
while my finger curls into my love
strokes the moist felicity

We spread our arms
in preliminary gestures of love
then close up
like a guilty sow bug
round as a cannonball
or an armadillo
plates of armor
to protect the soft inside
spongy as moss
or a vulva
secrete a case
to harden in
and petrify
die
Finally

I fall
into the invisible web
with fists of taffy
kick at the sticky fog at my feet
punch
the air
like a boxer too blinded to see
buzz
my wings
twist and turn
and pull and squirm
until breath spent
fall upside down in the net

like a fish on a hook
or a slab of carcass in a freezer
or a pink chicken
hung by its scaly legs
with plucked wings
and a skin film over its gray eyes
the skin on my heart
cold as the frost in a chemist's lab
makes your fingers sting to touch it
stick to it
finger
to plug up the hole in the flesh
and keep the hot fluid
of love's hunger back

Set me free set me free set me free
pluck me
out of the net
break the link
in the chain of slavery
put me
on a leaf
with all six of my legs
and I'll wipe the cotton candy
from my face
with my forearms
and rub the back of my head
with the second pair
and stretch out my hind legs
and scratch them together
to make static

Come together at the party
hook hands
play ring around the rosy
Don't let anybody leave
We will only be here a short time
a snap of fingers in eternity
Huddle under the warm covers
Wrap your arms around me
There's a narcotic hum in the air
can't you hear it?

Sleeeep
dozing off-stage
Sleeeep
sifting in between us
Slow chill
creeping over our flesh
like evening fog
It withers the lobes of our ears
Sleeeep
bringing nightmares and tears
Sleeeep
to spread over the land of our loving
those splashes and cries as we drown
Sleeeep
to lay you down

Sounds Out of the Inner Ear

Love
drips
like a beaded chain
of water
throbbing
like a drum
on the stone
of your heart

I can smell the wine
on your breath

We pump
to the same pulse
We shape
each other
We bend
in all the right places

The cords of your neck stand out
Sweat
makes a current of my arms
a creek of my prick
Sound
comes out of the inner ear
when you are near

The Pit of the Fruit

She lies in the dark light
in a room in my mind
She stretches back
and smiles
tiny wrinkles
at the sides of her mouth

She is thinking
of the baby I want in her body
She is thinking
of soft clouds
in which she floats
She is thinking
of an altar
on which she stands
with me
below her
looking up
through the parting in her breasts
at the underside
of her chin
her small mouth

She sees me
with her soft eyes
She sees me
with the shadows in her eyes
Her eyelid
is a wing
It softens her flight
It brings her back to me

She looks at me
from far back
in her
She looks
in me
She searches
for the source of the passion
in me
She knows
there is a light
Her gaze
is steady
She is serious
She knows
that I mean it
She knows
that if she looks deep enough
and long enough
she will pull me out
to her
that we will press together
cup mouths
switch tongues
that we will bend
to fit each other
that I
will lay myself down
on her breast
and cross necks

She knows
in the candlelight
all the secrets of the dark
She knows
all the strange cries
of all the jungle animals
She hears
the streams run
through the plantain leaves
the fan
of night wind
on a steamy bed of wild grass
She knows
where the seat of my heart lies
She sucks
at the pit of its fruit
and shares it with me

He Will Bleed Me Down to Serum for His Veins

He will bleed me down to serum for his veins
and pop me into his arm
He will sell me to the fence
at the corner grocery store
He will sell me to the rag sheeny
who trots his bony horse
through the alleys
swishing at flies
blinders on his eyes
He will sell me for a gun
to kill my father
and we'll all die in the end

I walk with my lost brother
in a strange city
He has been drinking
I try to find a place for him to rest
I ask people
old men
girls
They shake their heads
There is no room in this house for the dead
We stand alone in the street
my brother and I
and cry

Masked Men Hide Behind Doors

I walk around with a picture of her in my head
all the time
She stands by a table in white
hair down to her breasts and black
her face turned slightly
so as not to look at me
strands of hair thinning her cheeks

She is sad
because I have not offered to buy her a ring
but I will
She thinks
I don't want to live with her
but I do

Her face is inward now
wounded
its pale whiteness wrapped around itself
like a winding sheet
She thinks I do not trust her enough
but I might

She looks at me too sometimes
from down below
She looks up
from across the table at me

gray eyes by her black hair
cheeks of white
and rings my hand with her fingers
pleads with her eyes
to really love her
to trust her
tells me
she really loves me with them
and I want to

I walk around with a picture of her in my head
She lays on my couch and cups my hands
Her eyes are far away
She looks inward
at the pain she nurses in her breast
She gives suck to the sorrow
She settles her loins
She lets her legs rest
She does not curl her toes and make little cries
or squint her eyes
She holds down

She lets melancholy
seep in through her veins
and trickle through her body
like a map
She lets her sadness go
She lets it spread over her

Soon
she is submerged
and a shadow fills the room
rises like water
until the windows are black
and she has drowned me out

I walk around with a picture of her in my head
Masked men
hide behind doors
in black silhouettes
and peaked hats
and peek out
They stare at me
I wonder what they see?

Only the Winds of Her Moans in the Dark

All has come to an end
she screams on the phone
long moan
that makes the wires dance
buzz
in my ear
fear tingles
in every part of me

What have I done?
Why am I guilty?
I only want to love you
too
I am what I *do*
I commit no crime to look or care
I can stare
There is no sin in me
Jesus was wrong

Rain falls
in all the parts of me
Cloudy skies
no touch of blue
but blue inside
dark blue
dark blood
dark like a hood
hood over my head
so that I cannot see

Black over my eyes
ghosts
circle round me
An old man is dying
87 years long
he has lived on this earth
fathered
his last child at 58
He still has his mate
Why is it over?

Young man I am
I need my woman
woman with her lips open
and her legs
take my hand
and place it down there
to show me she cares
cup her hand over mine
and pierce my eyes
with the needle of her stare
She cares

Give this to you she says
without words
gestures
flock around us
hands
and blinking eyelashes
curl of her legs
lash herself to me

suck on the tip of my love
as I sink my heart in her
the shape of my tool
probe
to the center of our love
where the mists swirl
over the burning core of the earth
solar energy
spinning in circles inside her
fuse with my sperm
take the speck of my seed
and spin it in the hurricane
spin it in the hurricane
cyclone
without sound
only the winds of her moans
in the dark
Love me she says
Love you forever
only you love you
she says
her words crying
ripple of sobs
spreading out on the lake of the dark
before
we sink under
down in the depths
the hole of our yearning
the night of our sleep
joined together
forever
in the night

All has come to an end
The wall grows wide between us
space
that will tear our hearts apart
strings of blood
dripping across the crevasse
drying
like the dead meat of my dick
skinny
as a rawhide thong
it wiggles when I piss
like a worm
The surge is over
It is all over
All has come to an end.

Not Her

She speaks on the phone
her voice is low
She stays over there
at the end of the wave
where I can't touch her
or see her even
where she's safe from my influence
safe enough to hang up
and get away
She has to stay away
from me
Wish she didn't have to
but she does

She wants to find out
where she stands
She will either go nuts
or kill herself
kill herself
Maybe somebody else
will let me screw around
flirt with other girls
but not her
not her
not her

Not her she says
my love
at the other end of the line
where she gets off
purse and baggage
a book to read on the way
share with herself
Not her
my love
hitching off down the street
into the darkness
carrying my aching heart
pack it into the farthest corner
of her suitcase
wrapped in white paper
so soft
the blood spots come through
Not her
my love
blinking her eyes goodbye
one last signal
before she turns
Not her
moving off
back to me
back of her head
her face
she keeps for the future
signs off
not her
not her
not her

Not her
she will let me cry now
tears
stick to my spectacles
run down the glass
thick as honey
real as money
Not her
she walks out of my life
leaving the traces of hers
all around
an album on the phono
its jacket on the floor
the lid off the honey can
her slippers in the closet
her robe on a hook hanging in folds
without any body
There is nobody in there
no sail full of wind and smiles
so self-contained
in the closet
only the empty shapes of our lives
not her

Not her
she stands in the cold corners
where I shy from
huddle up when I go near
fear
shivers all over me
the corner
where the walls squeeze in

Not her
in this house that I can touch
really see
share the air with
Not her
anywhere to hold
but still dear with
in a radio by the bed she left
or her phono
and all her records
ballads
we shared before
now left behind
not her

Not her
I stand in this room
feeling only the want of her within me
the loss of her
around me
The sun shines
but coldly
There is a chill in the air
Cold Autumn comes in now
smiling
chilly but fair
Winter is near
frost on the car windows
in the mornings

Not her
around to keep me warm
in the rainy season
and the damp away
to play with my hair
Not her
Not her
Not her
Not her

The Blanket of Love Covers It All

Somewhere in the dark
her memory lies
lush kiss moist
she will suck you under
the blanket of love covers it all
Somewhere in the dark
she has met you
the last time
you were alone
without clothes to conceal you
the cry
in your fingertips
circling over
the small of her back

She lifted up to clamp you
between her thighs
carry you over
in the small boat of her snatch
over the bumpy wave
the splashing thrill in your face
whimpering
opening up all that
closing in
skin to skin
speaking
with her body
with blind fingers
a caress in motion
describing it all

The great wave of mistrust will drown it all
It rises
in the nights between
unseen
It sweeps into your dreams
fills the room
with its uneasy tide
lapping
into the corners of the ceiling
the tight cracks
of the wall
It covers all

She floats now
as if under water
bubbles
rising from her mouth
no sound
in her cry
beckoning
beckoning
knows she is going to die
hair streaming above her
currents in her eyes

There is only one life on this earth
and that is together
body to body

There is only the language of physical motion
the English
in a verb
the word
hard as rock
in space
Please
touch my face

Something Hangs About Us

We are born with our mothers
but we live
and die
alone
Spend most of our lives
shouting and gesturing at each other
through windows
as if there is a glass wall
in between

The one I love
whom I should be close to
whom I cleave to
share my body with
walks around outside me
as if in a dream
with a book in her hand
I see her face me
I see her mouth open
and her eyebrows rise
She looks right at me
Her lips move
Her eyes brighten
spark green
I wonder if something is wrong
But I cannot hear her

It is a lesson in futility
ghostly
as if we were already dead
but didn't know it

Something hangs about us
heavy in the air
you can almost taste
or touch
smell of body odor
when there is nobody
in the room
a stale scent of old clothes
in a closet
We see signs of it
sometimes
see hints of what's to come
in dreams
nightmares
the loss of self
with no return

I reach out for her
but can't touch
can't reach
Her mouth
opens wide
She seems to be
screaming

Last Tango in Paris

We were parting again for the umpteenth time
Last Tango in Paris
was playing its sweet melody
of hot lost love
and she was typing a letter
to the insurance company
then sealing it with a stamp
and her eyes
were bright and blue
close to her curly hair
as she was going out the door
looking in her purse
for her key or something
when it hit me
and I couldn't help but reach out
and put my hands on her shoulders
and stroke them
to keep the pain down

She came up smiling
and we closed
my arms
all the way around her
my head
down on her shoulder
my nose
on her shoulder strap
I could smell the leather

We rocked there to the music
in the middle of the floor
and I could feel her flat stomach against mine
touch mine with her breathing
our chests one
and I could feel her deep breaths
when I took my deep breaths
and I didn't want to ever break away
or leave her
or lose her
and the strings whined like sweet wind
and the sax was mournful
and husky
and mellow

Yet she had to go
and finally loosened her hold
but stopped
on the other side of the screen door
and leaned her nose against it
and I touched it with my finger
where it was warm on the wire
from her skin
while she stood there a while
with the sun streaming down
looking in

The Prophecy of Jonas

I had a star on my palm
could smell the dead skin and sweat
in the rioting crowd
listen to the love knock
of twisted bones
the clash
of tambourine and coin

I had a star on my palm

but if I waved it
I'd be quartered
from hind part to my toe!
crack my thumb!
make my mouth
a scar!

So I fled from my Lord 'cause
Why should He
wrench my arms on the cross
of prophecy

I bought me a boatman's fare
seeking the oblivion of foreign dust
the gloom of eventide air

But the waves clapped for my Lord's face
and I swooned in the bowels of a coffinwood ship
The Captain screamed in a storm tongue
so I cast my lot
for suffocation

and the sea
to set him free
He
was after me

Swallowed by a great fish
in the belly of Hell
with a flood in my soul
lament sounded like a rib echo
in the dampest cellars
of my father's house

I would unbraid the rancid odors of rotting meat
in the carnal street
in camel hair
and ashes

And the Lord spoke
and the fish vomited me
onto dry land

So I had to harken to the bid in my ear
the whine in the wind
open my palm
pocket my fear
mock the thrill
in the whore's song
spill out her breasts to the crowd
drench the gutter of her thighs
with my prayers and sighs
her thrashing hip
bang the drum
and jeer
the proud

And if they dared hit me
the shroud of His retribution
would smother
the glowing worms of their blood

So they cringed in the rattle of my tongue
wailed in the pinch of their sin
scrubbed off their evil
rubbed ash in their skin
The King choked on his robe
and bound the teeth of his dog
And the Lord saw
and spared them

Now I stood alone
prophet without a prophecy
My shadow bent with shame
My wreath of vindication
just a coiled wrath
of wrinkled grass
on my twisted brow

Had I paddled for three days and nights
to get my palm star slapped on my own cheek?
Then God
give me oblivion
under dung
and turf

Still I built a booth of derision and straw
a wind from the city
listened
for the grumble of His hailing stone

on the cracking marble
dampened
my brow
in an ivy shadow
taller
than a dame's leg
more crook
than her elbow
or her knee
then held up my hand
and waved my star

But the worm struck on the bitten leaf
and the sun broiled the juice in my head
the wind turned to sand

God
give me oblivion
under dung
and turf

Fool! said the Lord
a teaspoon could ladle the gilded pride
of that star on your palm
its creases of dust
onto the enameled plate of your greed
And *I* count the measures of a bard's song
the stroke of his baton
or stump his tongue

So when my martial spirit strains the air
strike my staff!
My colors billow black cyclone rage

But when the wind blows from the south
with a mild hymn
Chant
my praises
Sing
your bliss

For Shirley and All Those Other Black Girls Who Got Fired by Their Bosses

Suffering made him that way
He strikes the girl across the face
Slap sting that rings
clear to Moscow
reverberates
over the Siberian snow
White light
in my eyes
blinded
by the sun's jewels
air
nothing
that will fade with the shade

Her cry rings back
Black sound out of the cave
Moan
out of the center of our beings
where the gas is
and the bile
little volcanoes
erupting in puddles
in our spinning guts

She cries for all of us
Black sheep
we cook for Sunday dinner

The family
round the table
linen and silver
and smoky candles
women
in long evening dresses
pretty women
with jewels in their ears

She cries for them too
She cries for all the kids
bitten down by the fleas of the poor
thin wall of cold sweat
over their bodies
sweat
gray as their clothes
and the day
over their heads
kids running down back alleys
through the slime of Sunday mornings
with their mother
in a storefront church
and their father
in drunken mourning
wet towels over his head
his breath
the dead odor
of wilted gardenias
rats in the pantry
scurry of feet
patter out of the wall
behind the stove
Kill him with a sword
or a bayonet!

Fight him
for the flour and the food!

She cries for all of us

Black Girl
we hear your groan
we hear your wail
we feel the vibrations in your bones

Black Girl
we shall make it into song
song for all the lynched and the dead
for all the pickaninnies and gingerbread
for Uncle Tom too
and Malcolm X
for King the Prince of Peace
and George Jackson
and Huey Newton
and Eldridge Cleaver
all ground down
to lean hamburger
for the fed
They are dead

Black Girl
we hear your song
spirituals spun from frail cotton
and boll weevil
We hear the evil
Black Girl
We hear your song

Trip to the County Fair

Shack at the back of my yard
with your galvanized chimney
and your checkered door
Hello
from over here
on the steps of the back porch
in the shade
with the sun on my right toes
clouds
puffing out of your galvanized chimney
stripes
down your woodslats
dirt path
up to your door
through the yellow weeds
Great spray of soft cloud
in the blue sky
Hi!

I'm high on acid
and I'm talking to everything
It's all the same
House
trees
people
cows
all the same

I can feel the wind on my cheek
and my bare chest too
Bob of thorned vines to the breeze
Herb Alpert and his Tijuana Brass
behind me
and miniature roses
the size of my pinky nail
next to the porch
and I want to kiss them
and tell them all sorts of things
And when I look up
I see the shadows on the hills
floating
among the stems of the tree trunks
like lily pads
And my dog Sergie!
Oh my dog Sergie!
How pretty he is!
He curls down into a golden bowl of blond color
at my feet
tail wagging
thumping
Get up and bite my hand Sergie!
Saliva on it!
Crunch your teeth on my knuckles!
Hurray!

So we get in the car
and I've only been high five minutes
and just getting into it
I can feel the beautiful green fields come over me
Alfalfa!
Blow in my face!

Sway soft over my skin!
Tingle with the drone in the car in my head!
Yellow bus
pass by!

Oh look at that orange tractor go down the road!
Cowboy hat in the sun!
Grasshopper made of brass!
Glimmer!
Burn!
Catch fire like the yellow fields!
Blow!
Blow!

My chick's electric next to me
in her flowered dress
two blue buds in her hair
Thighs! Thighs!
Green eyes
wrinkle up at me and bat your lashes

but slow down
for the orange dirt grader
mechanical animal
chewing up the asphalt road
like a giant grasshopper

and watch out
for the cars on the highway
They'll catch you
in the wrong lane
on a curve
and crush you
under the iron grill

But look
at those pink flowers!
blooming out of the shale shoulder
at the side of the road!
and the cows in the field!
the calf
go bumping across
up and down with my head
buzzing
like the blue in the sky
Shimmer!
Shimmer!
Smoke discolors and feel the heat?
when you go by the lumber mill?
Look at that red reflector blink on that orange truck!
and the slow-down sign by a red flag!
the blue shirts on the two boys by the side of the road!
Bubble! Bubble!

Oh man
I'd like to put all those signs back there
by the roadside
in a poem
and make the reds and yellows
and greens and blues
and sky
all tingle in my head
Let the world vibrate around me!
join with my pulse beat!
knock on my temples!
Knock-Knock!
Sweat with my chin!
Bubble in the sun!
Have fun!

But in the city
I see color TV
I sweat on my chest
my chick's
flowering down the street next to me
in her miniskirt dress
We're going to drop by a store
She's going to buy something
We're following a lady's curlers
Yellow and green and red and blue
stuck to her head

All school things come from Penneys!
Shoes! Shoes!
Look at all the shoes!
White ones all over the place!
Moccasins!
Trunks!
Green trikes!
and yards and yards of draperies
blue and green flowers in profusion
spread out like a giant table cloth
vibrating
shimmer of cellophane
Blues and jagged Indian designs
lightning flash in reds and blues
blazing over me
Color!
Color!

A vibrating thrill passes over me
as these lines
fade into the pale lines
between the lines

Lines! Lines!
I can feel the air
bubbling around me
blowing dry wind
across the sweat on my back
and my neck
wet at the back
where the nape is
tingling over my scalp like mist

It rises out of my throat
a tingling
and I press up against the cigarette machine
feel the cool metal flat against my damp chest
I love everything
I even want to kiss the Coke machine
the summer checks that just walked by
swaying like a girl
blue eyes
slap of her heels on the floor
Blues! Blues!
Oh blue-lidded women!
Oh mascaraed eyes!
spread your soft skin against mine!
Women!
Women!
I'm being swamped by women!

Hear the air conditioner hum?
See that man go by in the handlebar mustache?
with the screwdrivers and pliers and hammers
hanging from his hips like six-guns?
that cowboy walk by?

But finally the fair
We get to the fair
Shade and wind
Flutter of silver and gold decorations
But you can tell it rained here the other night though
tire tracks through the mud straw and horseshit
a no-parking sign in front of two horses' asses
smell of manure

Chung
Peruvian Paso Pony
what's that I see in your eye?
your silver hide
with the mottled spots on it
like fish
swimming around under water

Cowboys
float around under their great big hats
A cloud apiece
on each head
proud as cocks
on the green rows of the benches

Clouds of smoke
rise up from a saw mill
as a horse lumbers by me
with a striped girl on its back
Cowgirls with blue-lidded eyes
sway by on swanky horses
Oh prance horse
cocky guy
around your mistress
snap that rope taut

draw it across the sky
and those green hills
in the background
with the blue water tank
Great swaying blue-breasted blond
let your locks blow in the wind
like a stream of smoke
swaying down the aisle
with a braid in the back

But the guitar wails and whines
for the little girl
who fell down with her horse
Now there's a crowd around
Listen to that guitar wail
See that red light
whirr on that red ambulance!
Crowds of people!
Cowboy hats and girls!
Girls in violet and blue!
There's a dark cloud over the rodeo
The ambulance is turning away with the girl
Hear the muffling wind?

I remember three things from my last rodeo
when I was a little boy
a white bull
that jumped over a blue convertible
an orangutang
with a purple ass and balls
and a skinny cowboy
who got bucked off a horse
and broke his neck

The transparent awning
stripes the sunburst from a storm cloud
and rakes over me
clatter of a garbage can
drone of a truck
Sun
Come down and shine on me
while I bask green in the fresh air
soft breeze
this green chair that I spread out in
one leg up
and let the girls walk by
clink-clink-clink of a slinky cowgirl
blond knot at the back of her head
sway of her blue-jeaned hips
and one brown eye
my way

Walk with that girl cowboy!
in your black hat and dark sunglasses
Cowboy and girl in the grass!
Girl with blond hair colored by the grass!
next to the blue stables the color of the sky!
try each other's faces
with your fingers!

Swarms of sunflowers
sway in and out like bees
in pulsating breaths
with the shadows on the hills

Mellow heat!
seep down through the center of my skull
and bubble out in sweat drops under my chin
rock to the beat
to the nifty rip-a-tip of the horn

Tijuana Brass
blow sweet and swinging over me!
Feel it in the breeze?
Feel it moisten my brow?
Flutter of the wind?
A soft blue all over us?
Color of the sky?

Hear the muted trumpet blow
with a hair-ruffling wind?
Lazy
ambling
sound
like blue smoke
on a hot day?
rising from the green moist grass
to the sky?
whiff of hay?

To My Wife To Tell Her Boss What I Do All Day

Dedicated to Al Young
and all starving poets

Tell him
I sit still in the sun
warming my sole
S-O-L-E

Tell him
I don't do anything
but sit down and read all day
stare at the page of your life
trace the chicken tracks
over the white void
deep as snow
footprints of darkness
black as this print
footsteps
into the nowhere ahead
down
into the final hole

Tell him
I think of this
all day!

Tell him
I *do* this!

Tell him
that's how I earn my keep!

Tell him
that I think about him too!
for him!

Tell him
that's something to *do* too!

More than one way to skin a cat!

One time
I would have been a priest
or better
a shaman
making the sun come up
every morning
giving it a reason to
chanting at it
to stay up
and help the kill
sucking in His will
spreading His vibes
to the whole tribe
especially to the hunters
Spears for their arms!
Arrows for their eyes!
who might die today!
against the wooly mammoth
and the saber tooth

I would have been him one time
Shaman
with knives in my hair
and tiger claws at my neck
red mud and fire ash
painted on my face
dancing around a drum
stomping and shouting
curing the sick
with one touch
of my finger
wand of electrical energy
a halo at its tip
saving the children
and the warriors
and suck the fever
out of the old

I would have been him one time
part of the tribe
helping them stay alive

In the Middle Ages maybe
I might have been a friar
like Saint Francis
or in France
like Villon
wandering around like a beggar
panhandling my poems
for a crown or two
half-out
of respectable society
and half-in
the big walls of the Church

too high for me
and sucking ass at a count's court
much too much to bear
Maybe I might have been that
in the Middle Ages

But not in our society
There's no place for me
Poetry doesn't sell
and I don't like to work
Can't see wasting all that time
for just money

I wanna stay free!
I wanna touch my soul every day!
I wanna spend my time
loving
what I do!

I don't wanna spend my time
working
for a living
I wanna spend my time
living
my work
I don't shirk
I spend all day at it
all the time
in the sunlight
and in the dark
I can't think of anything
better to do
Can you?

Two Loves

I have two loves
One is ginger
like midsummer
on white sand
and the stream's edge
Her current surrounds you
like air
when you move
as through water
She whirls
in little eddies
around
You float in her substance
She carries you along

Yet she sobs there
at the end of the line
and says she is sorry
for loving you too much
and yet
not enough

Her heart can hold you
but her body knows
she floats in no visions of yours
castles of light
on a seashore
She steps down
from no clouds to you

My other love
sings night songs
Moonlight
on her cheek
and soft shadows
in her eyes

She spreads her legs
to meet
the finger of my love
threading
the needle of her sex

I spin the womb on its tip
like a top
whirl of slow motion
that draws sound from its source
She sings
night songs
I listen
for her voice on the phone
Every time it rings
I hold my breath
expect
the husky sound
the deep
resonance
from down in the throat

Yet I know
that she will not call
that the tactics of her war
says no
to that with me
Jealousy
rings her thoughts
curls
her ring finger

She holds her love
to her
hugs it
a small pinpoint
of fire
that bleeds
in a tiny
trickle

Love Letter

I should have written this poem
a couple of days ago
when I first got here
and your image
was fresh before me
when your face
was all I could see
all day

The light of the window
behind you
and the pale softness
of brown
that enveloped you
the brown turtleneck
that clung so close
that showed your small bones
the delicacy
of them

and the way your hair
done up in back in a bun
carried this soft tone of brown
The shadows in the room
and the gray day outside
seemed tan too

Then
when the catlike shape of your face
held me
when I saw it
everywhere I turned
when I talked
to someone else
and saw you
when each secret
thought was you
when my mind
hung in some separate chamber
in a room
on a third floor
overlooking a park
with a sketching on the window
and you faced me
kneeled down on the bed
below me
and the light
seemed to wrap around your head
with your hair
so that the stems of your neck showed
and all the fine bones
that fit together
so well

then
I should have written this poem

then
you would have believed me

Great Big Pink Cement Trucks
A Love Poem

I like great big pink
cement trucks
dusted
a pastel shade
by sacks & sacks
of powdery cement

& I like the concrete
that's crusted
all around the hubcaps
& the spokes
of the wheels
& spattered
on the truck sides
& even around the mouth of the chute
at the back
though the driver washes it off
with a small hose
attached to the cement mixer
after he dumps each load

And I like the curve
of the great big cylinder
the way it sits
on end
behind the cab
& tips
like a falling top

when it turns
the slush inside
the drum sound
when I beat it
with the sides of my fists

And I like the great big wheels
I like to feel
the treads
of the giant tires
with my hands
hook my fingers
into the deep grooves
& when I stretch my arms wide
rub the hollows
of my palms
on the thick
rubber
edges

The Professor and the Lumberjack

The Professor of English
and the lumberjack
met in a bar
orange tea and bourbon
gin grin
and the knuckle crunch
of eye teeth
spectacles
and nuts

Two fifths later
the Professor
took the lumberjack home
and took off his clothes
and hurt the lumberjack's feelings

But the lumberjack stayed
and took his clothes off
flexed his muscle
tied the Professor to the bed
whipped him with his own belt
beat him
into an orgasm
of sperm and blood
swoon and scream
coming
and dying
and then
pissed on him

They Have Come to Steal My Woman

They have come to steal my woman!
All those mothers!
I see her through the window
throwing her daughter's clothes in her suitcase
She bends down
and I can only see her gray hair
But when she straightens up
she is not a mother
She doesn't have the face of a mother
Mothers
don't have such bony faces
Mothers
have flesh in their cheeks
Mothers'
necks quiver
Mothers
have smiling lights in their eyes
Mothers
love sons too
Young sons
Handsome sons
Sons with big smiles
She is not a mother

She has gray hair though
and the tanned skin of the very rich
golden brown
pale as toast
and blue hair

blue
like her eyes
that blue
whitened by the snow
and distilled
by sitting still
in the sun
that blue
blue as water and just as clear
blue
the color of silver coin
blue
like her veins

She grabs her daughter by the arm
My woman she says
must go home
home
to someone who can support her
and send her
to Europe
to forget
me
to Europe
to celebrate her ancestors' birthdays
on holidays
to Europe
where she can forget
me

I see
my woman's dress is up
I stroke her snatch
I tell her
not to cry
I tell her
not to worry
I tell her
that it's all right
and look in her face
to see
how she
feels about it
But she
has her shoulder
against my chest
and her face
turned
as if she cannot look
at me
I push her back
to see

This is not my woman
My woman
was soft and round-cheeked and pretty
This woman
has her hair pulled back
and a sharp chin
and a black and white polka dot dress

This is not my woman
My woman
is with me
in me
My woman
is not with her mother

All the mothers
come to steal my woman
They shake their fingers
and flutter their lips
They sway their hips
They shoo me
away from their babies

The Coffee Shop

Chess men and empty chairs
guys and girls sitting around
lamp light
shadows on the floor
but some other light
draws us here
memories of a lost Eden
crowd around

But the cave men of France
knew what an arrow was
They lived on more than roots
and plucked fruit
They killed and stuck together
just to survive
They survived

Loneliness
draws us to the light here
flame about which we flicker
magnetic pull of hollow
to hollow
wink of an eyelash quick as life

Strange birds like me
sit at tables and stare
wanting to care
a ring on a finger
finger on a knee
flicks at me
I see
though feeling
eludes me

Picture Smoke on a Mirror

She gave me that word
long ago
when we first kissed
and she wondered
if it would last
She did not think
I believed it
and now she will not speak it

Behind the black glint
of the stone in her eyes
I see nothing

Picture smoke on a mirror
clinging like adhesive
to its own cloud
and you see what I see
when I see
her face

All About Sex

At least we're hung up on tits in America
not on plastic Virgin Marys
glued onto dashboards
like the Spaniards
though you can't touch either one

& I wonder if we'll ever have
a truly natural & happy sex life
on this fucked-up earth?

It's possible
in some future time
when the atom bomb has become a buddy
& out of the polar icecaps
make power to green the rest of the earth
make an Eden for everybody
& nobody'd have to work & support babies
so who cares who
the father is
like the Polynesians
before Moby Dick got there
I mean Herman Melville

& where does James Brown go from here?
the rock & talk way he makes music
down home
hums like a throaty saxophone
with words
all about sex
Do you love me?
Yes I love you
Ain't that a groove?

To Sergie My Sweet Old Dog

This is the reality now Sergie
this mound of earth
under the camellia bush
with a bouquet of orange poppies
alive at its foot
the shade that sprinkles it
even in the sunshine
There will always be sprinkles on this gravesite
summer or winter
raining or shining
I sprinkle it now with my tears

One of the poppies is dying though
the brown bud of a withered face
smiles out
through the bent strands
of its petals
peeking up through the bent brim
of an old straw hat
though his bloom's all gone
like yours was
these last two years

I suck in air to ease the cramp in my gut
Miki my Japanese puppy
nibbles some grass on your grave
A bird trill thrills me
from the big bush over your head
The sun warms me
The long branches of a thin plum tree

burst into beads of green buds
and rows of buttons of white flowers
Poppies
spin like a fleet of flying suns
over the green clover
in the speckled shade
of a knobby pear tree

This is the reality
Sergie
You down in the deep damp hole
the rain seeping into your ears
trickling through the fears
a slow movement
of flesh and bone
back to silt
back to the mud of my back yard
back to these earth clods
spongy with the whole night's rain
This is my pain

This is the reality
Sergie
dogchain
hanging from the doorknob
red cross of its rabies tag
and green heart
of its license

a breeze on me
shadow of leaves
flickering on my page
no you around
on top of the ground

No Sergie
to sniff noses with
no sweet
and earthy canine smell

The reality is
there is
no trace of you
here
aside from this small mound of dirt
in the yard
and the warm coral
of my brain
the pain
in my chest

This is the reality
Sergie

My Lovely

For Melinda

I've learned how to live under pressure
have joy
in paranoia
dance
kick my heels
shake my shoulders
wiggle my hips
keep time with my feet
make rhythm
with my whole body
all at once
every part pulsing to the song
the beat
of the drum
spirit
rising up
out of the body
in romance
and just plain feeling good
the thumping heart in tune
the sweat
breathing bubbles out all over
panting like my breath

At full moon
the moon glows
the cool fire
spinning in the sky
dripping love
in a halo
the color of a rainbow
misty bed of clouds
streaking down
over your head

Snow is cold like the moon
glow of metal
like the color
of her eyes in the night
like her hair
cool yellow
like the moon
like her face
a tiny drop of ivory
chill dew
congealed
in the cold

Somewhere inside
the fire burns
like the moon
both hot and cold
eternal paradox
There is always more than what you see
the cold moon glows hot
with feeling

cool melancholy
rising to a slow burn
the electric flame
of the sun
glancing off the surface
of stone metal
cold metal
swimming with ions
and magnetism
ball of hot ice
you can cup in your palm

The blood bubbles too
in the deepest part
in the heart
of her
where the sadness is
the untold story
the blossom
still unbloomed
tight bud
bent like your finger
tight
as your knuckle
pale and wrinkled
as your knuckle
the blood bubbles there
little pops on the surface
like a fish bite
searching
for the bait

The worm lives
but only the warmth of my palm
can caress it
into color
into a butterfly's wings
shivering
with freedom
breathing
with slow breaths
like a fan
Only my lips
can kiss it into color
into flame
prod it
into flight
broken flutter over the lawn
like a flying flower
quick as a bat
the wings flicker with color
pale gold and orange
with a green lining
they are climbing
up
into the sun

Black Star Sparkling Between White Thighs

In the hollow of the room
in the lap of the bed
in the black star sparkling
between her thighs
in the bag we have wrapped around each other
that tissue of feeling
that envelops us
that sheathes
our curling arms
that net
that holds us
and hangs suspended
like a hammock from the sky
in the swaying of our love
in the rocking of our hearts
in the darting of our hummingbird tongues
the sweet taste
waters my palate
scorches my skin
and I smell the odor of sea
and mildew
and forget her tears

For there are no tears dropping here
in the dark light that fuses limbs
only the white star of sperm
that moans into form
as we melt
into each other

The Streetwalker

Somewhere
on the curvature of the earth
a few streetlights on a dark hillside
a slim girl in black
steps out to me
a dark curl on her temple

She wears a black hat
with a rose in it
and a mole on her cheek
the color of rose
on her lips
her mouth in shadow
the light falls
on her chin

But I will not kiss those lips

for if she should speak
flowers
would come out her mouth
and there would be
thorns
on them
and their fragrance
a breath
with the hint of tequila

She bares her teeth now
and in the gleam
between pink and pink
petal and petal
the tip of her tongue shows
She curls it along her lip
on the underside of the top one

Between the tip of that tongue
and the fold between her legs
stars sputter
and the lights on my hillside
go out

Mouth to Mouth

Sand in my heart
that part
when rubbed
that becomes a pearl
that part
where she fights me
holds me off
won't kiss me

See the heron in the sand?
Sea gull soar over the rock?
Slow splash of waves?

Give me that gift
without weighing in balance
what's at stake
like my dog does
like I do
to you

Bite my lips
Caress them with your tongue
Close your eyes
be mouth to mouth with me

If Only from the Stroke of Tenderness

Dedicated to Paladin and all other fascists

Fascists everywhere!
Political fascists!
Sexual fascists!
Homosexual fascists!
Mother fascists!
Sister fascists!
Brother fascists!
Biker fascists!
Fascist in black pants and boots
and one black glove
on his right hand
tattoo on his chest
poking his pale arm up
through an armless vest
to Zieg Heil
bear fuzz
growing on his back
cat fur
all over his face
porcupine quills
for hair

A funny fascist
stomping all around
not much bigger than his boot himself
heavy black eyebrows
thin body
jabbing that black glove up in the air
shouting at the top of the scale

screaming about death and dying
violence
smash you in the face
the true sin and nature of man
man the selfish beast
man who straddles his woman
and sticks her with his spear
till the blood squirts out

Man the killer!

And what is it all about but the hunt anyway?
to keep yourself alive at another man's expense
women
slaving at your shoes
women
to step on
to squish the musical notes from
press down on their bodies with your boots
to make the spurs jingle

Little fascist
what are you doing all the shouting about?
I think I hear you singing!
Sounds like a song to me!
Song from out of your guitar body
strum your thin ribs through your skin!
Song
out of your anguish
the cry
which makes your chest creak
the wind
out of your heart

the care
in you
the part
that wants to cry
if only from the stroke
of tenderness
tenderness
dear as your blood
dear
as you are to yourself
inside
in all the parts of you
the part
that loves
the part
that makes it all worthwhile
the part
that sees beauty
needs beauty
sucks on beauty
craves beauty
beauty in a sunset
beauty in a woman's face
or her breasts
the shape of her box
little triangle of bush
with the God's eye in it
the hole
of eternity
the passport
to forever
if only
for a minute

shivering minute
minute shared with another
minute
within another
minute
with
another minute
all being more
than one minute
without any parts
total harmony
total bliss
euphoria
escape
essence
the absolute

That's more than just killing
little fascist
That's more than always being one up
getting the jump on
There's more than one side to a coin
little fascist
I kill for my food
just like you do
though I use a can opener instead of a gun
or a carving knife
I bleed the poor little pigs
and cushiony sheep myself
there's no denying that
But not all of me wants to kill
One part
wants to love

One part
takes off in flight like the cooing doves
that flutter
like soft shadows
in the branches
One part
cares!
One part
knows
what makes it feel good!
One part
gets there!
One part
is more than you are even to yourself!
The spirit
that glows from you
like a halo!
like Jesus!
like the sun!

All beings share in it!
have it!
burn with it!
Energy of the soul!
Electricity!
Magnetism!
Love!
Feeling!
Emotion!
The spirit
that can reach out
and touch another!

feel
another!
lift you
out of yourself!
leave some traces
of what you are
behind
in those poems you write
little fascist
poet
brother
fellow survivor
spinning around
in empty space
like
me

Easter Sun Day on Red River or Death and Resurrection in Arizona 1983

For Claire and Jesus

The Red River turns bloody
after it passes the slaughterhouse

Wind polishes the red cliff to a shine
in the sun
smooths all the caves and hollows
into seashells

We go to see the Grand Canyon
across this rocky desert
flocked with stunted trees
Flocks of clouds
sail on the edges of blue

I want you
I want to feel the pull between us
wire-taut
singing

cushion the heart of your lips

taste you

The sun shines now but last night
we had to run from the blizzard
down out of the Rockies
over the ice on Raton Pass
in the dark

snowflakes
dusting our back bumper
curling
into strange icy worms
on our rear window

We drove toward the stars
and the moon
lingering ahead
behind a black cloud

We drove down
out of the ice mountains
into the baked land of the sun

on a sunny Easter morning
snow packed
on the pass behind

Now I feel liberated
Now I feel freed
Now I feel the need
to touch

you

Wyoming Is an Indian Name

Crossing the plateau of Wyoming by van,
March 31, 1983

Hello on your birthday Claire
I speak to the rocks of Wyoming
The Indian call haunts
the snow-speckled hills
Sculptured stratifications of rock
sing of the ages
when this plateau
was an inland sea
I see the bottom of the ocean
pressed against
the bottom of the snow-leaded sky

It leans on me
heavily
smothering me
like a hot blanket
without you

I take deep breaths
to make sure I live
Loneliness
drove the pioneer women of the plains
mad

All day
squeezed between the dry earth
and the sky
for years
can make you cry

Wyoming!
the Indian chants
but his call fades
like a thin spiral of signal smoke
smothered
by miles and miles of flat dirt
that spread out
in a tightening circle
around me
trapping
this shell of a flesh man
in this hull
of a steel car
too far
to touch you
on your birthday

I know what I was doing
thirty-one years ago
on this day Claire
but I didn't know then
a woman was being born
that I'd love now
in this
far
future

The Elemental Killing of the Fish

For Art García

He hangs a live clam
a pulpy mess
from the end of a hook
with a stone's weight lead sinker
and lobs it
off the side
with a short swing
of the pole
away from him
washing
the blood from his hands

–There is no guilt here
He just remembers how to kill
I use
a can opener–

The line beads
into the water
like the single strand
of a spider's web

Stars of sunlight
float on the wave
She spreads her thighs
to the light
A bird
wings
over
shaped
like a stuka plane
arcs
into a boomerang
above us
A motorboat
roars by
The waves
rock us
tip us
from side
to side

It stole
his bait